Demystifying Quantum Ecosystem: Algorithms for Leaders

Volume I

AF527589

Authors

Sanjana Rajeshkumar Gupta

Dr. Satyam Priyadarshy

Global Quantum Intelligence, LLC

ZORBA BOOKS

ZORBA BOOKS

Published by Zorba Books, March 2026
Website: www.zorbabooks.com
Email: info@zorbabooks.com
Author Name: Sanjana Rajeshkumar Gupta, Dr. Satyam Priyadarshy, Global Quantum Intelligence
Copyright ©: Sanjana Rajeshkumar Gupta, Dr. Satyam Priyadarshy, Global Quantum Intelligence

Title: Demystifying Quantum Ecosystem: Algorithms for Leaders

Printbook ISBN: 978-93-5896-323-6
Ebook ISBN: 978-93-5896-694-7

All rights reserved. No part of this book may be reproduced or transmitted in any form or by any means, electronic or mechanical, except by a reviewer. The reviewer may quote brief passages, with attribution, in a review to be printed in a magazine, newspaper, or on the Web—without permission in writing from the copyright owner.

The publisher under the guidance and direction of the author has published the contents in this book, and the publisher takes no responsibility for the contents, its accuracy, completeness, any inconsistencies, or the statements made. The contents of the book do not reflect the opinion of the publisher or the editor. The publisher and editor shall not be liable for any errors, omissions, or the reliability of the contents of the book.

Any perceived slight against any person/s, place or organization is purely unintentional.

Zorba Books Pvt. Ltd. (opc)
Sushant Arcade,
Next to Courtyard Marriot,
Sushant Lok 1, Gurgaon – 122009, India

Printed in India

DEDICATION

This work is dedicated to the visionaries and pragmatic leaders who look beyond the distractions of the "quantum winter" or "quantum hype." It is intended for those committed to guiding their organizations through the second quantum revolution with clarity, purpose, and unwavering focus on fostering a resilient and intelligent future, with a foundational understanding expressed in simple terms.

DISCLAIMER

This book is intended for informational and educational purposes only to assist leaders in navigating the quantum transition. The technical definitions and references provided are subject to the evolving nature of quantum research, and readers should consult specific experts for implementation-level decisions.

Contents

Preface

The shift from the classical to the quantum era is more than just about increased computing power; it's an exciting new way of thinking about how we process information, safeguard our assets, and explore the nature of reality itself. For many years, quantum mechanics was mainly explored by theoretical physicists and dedicated researchers. Now, it's moving out of the labs and into the boardroom, marking a big step forward. As we approach a major digital transformation worldwide, leaders will need a new kind of upskilling one that makes complex ideas easier to understand and emphasizes their strategic importance.

Demystifying Quantum Ecosystem: Algorithms for Leaders, Volume I, stems from the need to connect advanced quantum theory with practical industry applications. As a practitioner navigating digital disruption with exponential technologies in complex sectors like Oil and Gas and Energy, I have noticed that the main obstacle to adoption is not just technical complexity but also a lack of conceptual clarity. Leaders don't need to solve complex equations; they need to understand why certain mathematical methods, algorithms fit into their organizations' near-term future.

This book is written in straightforward, everyday language to remove the confusing terminology of "qubits" and "entanglement" and instead focus on what these tools really *do*.

We explore the various algorithms that define the full quantum field:

- **Computing algorithms,** such as Shor's and Grover's, represent a seismic shift in how we factor numbers and search through vast amounts of data.
- **Quantum Machine Learning**: Techniques like Quantum Principal Component Analysis enable us to find significant patterns in high-dimensional data.
- **Communication and Security**: Protocols like BB84 that fundamentally alter the risk profile of our cybersecurity infrastructure.
- **Hybrid Solutions**: Tools like the Variational Quantum Eigensolver (VQE) are built for the near-term hardware we currently have, helping bridge the gap between classical limits and quantum potential.

The "Ecosystem" in the title is intentional. Quantum technology doesn't exist in isolation; it is part of a larger "TIGER" framework encompassing Technology, Innovation, Growth, Efficiency, and Resilience, as defined by Priyadarshy. In industries such as Mining, Oil and Gas, and Energy, where AI-driven solutions are being implemented, the quantum algorithms discussed here will be the key drivers of future competitive advantage. When it comes to communications, whether on Earth or interstellar, quantum algorithms will soon provide secure, efficient, and resilient communication channels.

This guide helps leaders ask, "What is possible?" and "When is it relevant?" It aims to empower confident leadership through the quantum transition. The quantum age is here; the time to lead is now.

Dr. Satyam Priyadarshy

CEO, Reignite Future

Board Advisor, Global Quantum Intelligence, LLC

Visiting Chair Professor, IIT Bombay

About this Book

The rapid development of quantum technologies signifies a fundamental change in our computational landscape, moving beyond the constraints of classical physics to harness principles such as superposition and entanglement. For organizational leaders, the difficulty is in navigating a field often obscured by technical jargon and speculative hype. This thorough document acts as a strategic dictionary, translating complex quantum algorithms for appropriate solutions in quantum era decision-making.

Within these pages, you will discover the fundamental elements of the quantum ecosystem, from **Shor's Algorithm**, which redefines digital security, to the **Variational Quantum Eigensolver (VQE)**, which is already changing material science and drug discovery. Each entry offers a high-level overview of the algorithm's purpose, along with authoritative academic references to ensure a strong technical foundation.

This guide is more than just a list of terms; it functions as a roadmap for the quantum transition. By explaining these algorithms in simple, everyday language, leaders can effectively steer their organizations toward a future marked by quantum-enhanced efficiency, security, and innovation. Whether your focus is on safeguarding global communication networks or optimizing complex industrial supply chains, this alphabetical glossary provides the clarity needed to lead confidently in the quantum era.

The Foundational Algorithms of Quantum

Abelian Hidden Subgroup Problem

This algorithm finds hidden patterns in functions where the symmetry follows simple, commutative rules (where the order of operations doesn't matter). It serves as a unified framework that includes well-known methods such as Shor's algorithm, enabling quantum computers to detect these structures with exponential efficiency.

- **Reference**: Jozsa, R. (1998). Quantum algorithms and the Fourier transform. *Proceedings of the Royal Society of London. Series A: Mathematical, Physical and Engineering Sciences*, 454(1969), 323–337.

Adiabatic Quantum Optimization (AQO)

This method begins with a simple quantum system and gradually evolves it into a more complex one, where the final "rest" state signifies the optimal solution to an optimization problem. It depends on the physics of remaining in the lowest possible energy state throughout the process to ensure accuracy.

- **Reference**: Farhi, E., Goldstone, J., Gutmann, S., Lapan, J., Lundgren, A., & Preda, D. (2001). A quantum adiabatic evolution algorithm applied to random instances of an NP-complete problem. *Science*, 292(5516), 472–475.

Amplitude Amplification

This technique uses quantum interference to repeatedly enhance the probability of a desired state while reducing that of undesired ones, ensuring the correct answer is found more reliably. It acts as a broad mathematical generalization of the specific search process used in Grover's algorithm.

- **Reference**: Brassard, G., Høyer, P., Mosca, M., & Tapp, A. (2002). Quantum amplitude amplification and estimation. *Contemporary Mathematics*, 305, 53–74.

Amplitude Estimation

This algorithm determines the unknown probability of a specific outcome by combining amplitude amplification with phase estimation. It offers a quadratic speedup compared to classical methods, making it a powerful tool for complex simulations and financial risk analysis.

- **Reference**: Brassard, G., Høyer, P., Mosca, M., & Tapp, A. (2002). Quantum amplitude amplification and estimation. *Contemporary Mathematics*, 305, 53–74.

BB84 Protocol

A fundamental quantum communication protocol for Quantum Key Distribution (QKD) enables two parties to create a secure cryptographic key using photon polarization. It relies on the principle that any eavesdropper's observation will disturb the quantum state, exposing their intrusion.

- **Reference**: Bennett, C. H., & Brassard, G. (1984). Quantum cryptography: Public key distribution and coin tossing. *Proceedings of IEEE International Conference on Computers, Systems and Signal Processing*, 175–179.

Bernstein-Vazirani Algorithm

This algorithm is designed to solve a "hidden string" problem, identifying a secret *n*-bit string in a single attempt. While a standard computer would need to ask *n* queries, this quantum approach achieves a linear speedup by leveraging interference to reveal the entire string at once.

- **Reference**: Bernstein, E., & Vazirani, U. (1997). Quantum complexity theory. *SIAM Journal on Computing*, 26(5), 1411–1473.

Boson Sampling

This algorithm simulates how identical particles of light (photons) behave as they pass through a complex network of beam splitters. It is a specialized task designed to demonstrate "quantum supremacy" because computing photon distributions is very challenging for classical computers.

- **Reference**: Aaronson, S., & Arkhipov, A. (2011). The computational complexity of linear optics. *Proceedings of the 43rd Annual ACM Symposium on Theory of Computing*, 333–342.

Chopped Random Basis (CRAB) Algorithm

A quantum optimal control algorithm that employs a randomized basis of functions to optimize control pulses for quantum state preparation and gate operations. It is especially effective for systems where the exact Hamiltonian is not fully known.

- **Reference**: Doria, P., Caneva, T., Calarco, T., & Montangero, S. (2011). Optimal control technique for many-body quantum dynamics. *Physical Review Letters*, 106(19), 190501.

Class Group

This algorithm calculates the structure of the "class group," which explains how unique factorization breaks down in certain mathematical systems. Quantum computers can efficiently identify these complex structures, offering insights into the fundamental properties of algebraic numbers.

- **Reference**: Hallgren, S. (2005). Fast quantum algorithms for computing the unit group and class group of a real quadratic field. *Proceedings of the 37th Annual ACM Symposium on Theory of Computing*, 468–474.

Collision Finding

This algorithm searches for two distinct inputs that produce the same output when processed by a function, a task crucial for testing digital security. Quantum computers utilize a combination of Grover-style search and memory to find these "collisions" much faster than traditional brute-force methods.

- **Reference**: Brassard, G., Høyer, P., & Tapp, A. (1997). Quantum algorithm for the collision problem. *arXiv preprint quant-ph/9705002*.

Deutsch-Jozsa Algorithm

A deterministic quantum algorithm that determines if a black-box Boolean function is constant or balanced using only a single query. It provides a formal proof of exponential speedup over classical deterministic algorithms for this specific problem.

- **Reference**: Deutsch, D., & Jozsa, R. (1992). Rapid solution of problems by quantum computation. *Proceedings of the Royal Society of London. Series A*, 439(1907), 553–558.

Diffusion Monte Carlo (DMC)

A quantum Monte Carlo method that uses a stochastic projector to evolve a trial wavefunction in imaginary time, effectively filtering out higher-energy states to find the ground state. It is widely used in quantum chemistry to simulate many-body electronic systems.

- **Reference**: Foulkes, W. M. C., Mitas, L., Needs, R. J., & Rajagopal, G. (2001). Quantum Monte Carlo simulations of solids. *Reviews of Modern Physics*, 73(1), 33.

Discrete Logarithm

Similar to factoring, this quantum algorithm finds the exponent **x** in the equation $g^x = h \pmod{n}$ much faster than any known classical method. Because many modern cryptographic protocols rely on the hardness of this problem, quantum computers could render those systems insecure.

- **Reference**: Shor, P. W. (1997). Polynomial-time algorithms for prime factorization and discrete logarithms on a quantum computer. *SIAM Journal on Computing*, 26(5), 1484–1509.

Element Distinctness

This algorithm checks a list to see if every item is unique or if at least two items are identical. By using a specialized quantum walk, it can identify duplicates in a large dataset significantly faster than classical sorting or comparison methods.

- **Reference**: Ambainis, A. (2007). Quantum walk algorithm for element distinctness. *SIAM Journal on Computing*, 37(1), 210–239.

Formula Evaluation

This is a general method for computing the result of a large mathematical or logical formula represented as a tree of operations. Quantum computers can explore all potential branches of the tree simultaneously, providing a faster way to solve complex logic problems.

- **Reference**: Ambainis, A., Childs, A. M., Reichardt, B. W., Špalek, R., & Zhang, S. (2010). Any AND-OR formula can be evaluated in $O(N^{1/2+o(1)})$ steps on a quantum computer. *SIAM Journal on Computing*, 39(6), 2513–2530.

Gauss Sum Estimation

This algorithm approximates the values of special mathematical sums involving complex numbers and modular arithmetic. These sums are critical in number theory and physics, and quantum computers can estimate them with a precision that classical computers struggle to match.

- **Reference**: van Dam, W., & Seroussi, G. (2002). Efficient quantum algorithms for estimating Gauss sums. *arXiv preprint quant-ph/0207131*.

Gaussian Boson Sampling (GBS)

A more advanced variation of boson sampling that uses "squeezed" states of light to simplify the experimental setup while remaining computationally hard for classical machines. It is particularly useful for solving real-world mathematical problems, such as finding patterns in graphs or optimizing complex networks.

- **Reference**: Hamilton, C. S., et al. (2017). Gaussian boson sampling. *Physical Review Letters*, 119(17), 170501.

Gradient Ascent Pulse Engineering (GRAPE) Algorithm

An iterative optimal control algorithm that calculates the gradient of a performance figure (like gate fidelity) with respect to control field amplitudes to find the most efficient pulse sequence. It is a standard tool for implementing high-fidelity gates in superconducting and NMR quantum computers.

- **Reference**: Khaneja, N., et al. (2005). Optimal control of coupled spin dynamics: Design of NMR pulse sequences by gradient ascent algorithms. *Journal of Magnetic Resonance*, 172(2), 296–305.

Graph Isomorphism

This refers to a set of methods used to determine whether two complex networks are identical in structure, even if their visual layouts differ. Quantum methods, particularly those involving quantum walks, are being explored to solve this task much faster than classical brute-force approaches.

- **Reference**: Aharonov, D., & Gottlieb, A. (2003). A quantum algorithm for the Hamiltonian cycle problem. *Foundations of Physics*, 33(7), 1033–1050.

Grover's Algorithm

A quantum search algorithm that provides a quadratic speedup for finding a specific element in an unstructured database of size *N*. It works by iteratively applying the Grover Operator to amplify the probability amplitude of the target state.

- **Reference**: Grover, L. K. (1996). A fast quantum mechanical algorithm for database search. *Proceedings of the 28th Annual ACM Symposium on Theory of Computing*, 212–219.

Hamiltonian Simulation

This technique models how a quantum system (such as a drug molecule or a new metal) evolves by mimicking its natural laws. It is considered one of the most promising applications for early quantum computers in chemistry and material science.

- **Reference**: Lloyd, S. (1996). Universal quantum simulators. *Science*, 1073–1078.

Hidden Shift Problem

This algorithm identifies the exact amount by which one function has been "slid" or shifted relative to another identical function. It is a specialized symmetry problem in which quantum computers can determine the shift with far fewer queries than classical systems.

- **Reference**: van Dam, W., Hallgren, S., & Ip, L. (2003). Quantum algorithms for some hidden shift problems. *Proceedings of the 14th Annual ACM-SIAM Symposium on Discrete Algorithms*, 489–498.

Hidden Subgroup Problem

This is a high-level mathematical framework that uses quantum properties to find "hidden symmetries" or repeating structures inside a function. It is considered the "grand architecture" of quantum computing because many famous algorithms, like Shor's, are actually just specific versions of this problem.

- **Reference**: Lomont, J. S. (2004). The quantum hidden subgroup problem. *arXiv preprint quant-ph/0411037*.

Matrix Elements & Multiplicity Coefficients

This algorithm computes the complex numerical properties of symmetry groups, which describe how physical systems change under rotations or shifts. These calculations are vital for quantum chemistry and particle physics, where quantum computers can model group interactions more naturally than classical hardware.

- **Reference**: Bacon, D., Childs, A. M., & van Dam, W. (2005). From quantum Schur transform to quantum Clebsch-Gordan transform. *Proceedings of the 46th Annual IEEE Symposium on Foundations of Computer Science*, 369–378.

NAND Tree Evaluation

This algorithm determines the final output of a complex decision tree built entirely from NAND logic gates. Quantum computers use a "scattering" approach to evaluate these trees, allowing them to find the correct result faster than any classical program could by checking branches individually.

- **Reference**: Farhi, E., Goldstone, J., & Gutmann, S. (2008). A quantum algorithm for the Hamiltonian NAND tree. *Theory of Computing*, 4(1), 169–190.

Non-Abelian Hidden Subgroup Problem

This represents a more complex version of the symmetry problem, in which the order of operations can significantly change the result. Solving this efficiently is a major goal in quantum research, as it could enable cracking complex codes and solving hard graph problems.

- **Reference**: Grigni, M., Schulman, L., Vazirani, M., & Vazirani, U. (2001). Quantum algorithms for the non-Abelian hidden subgroup problem. *Proceedings of the 33rd Annual ACM Symposium on Theory of Computing*, 68–77.

Pell's Equation

This algorithm finds integer solutions to equations of the form $x^2 - Dy^2 = 1$ using quantum period-finding techniques. Quantum computers provide an exponential speedup for this task, which is historically significant in number theory and requires finding very large integers.

- **Reference**: Hallgren, S. (2007). Polynomial-time quantum algorithms for Pell's equation and the principal ideal problem. *Journal of the ACM (JACM)*, 54(1), 4-es.

Primality Proving

This procedure uses quantum-enhanced logic to verify, with certainty, whether a given large number is prime and to generate a mathematical certificate of that proof. Quantum computers can perform this verification faster than classical probabilistic tests for extremely large numbers.

- **Reference**: Agrawal, M., Kayal, N., & Saxena, N. (2004). PRIMES is in P. *Annals of Mathematics*, 781–793.

Principal Ideal Problem

This quantum algorithm determines if a given ideal in a number field is "principal" and identifies the generator that defines its structure. It leverages quantum algorithms for continuous hidden subgroup problems to solve a task that is classically computationally intensive.

- **Reference**: Hallgren, S. (2007). Polynomial-time quantum algorithms for Pell's equation and the principal ideal problem. *Journal of the ACM (JACM)*, 54(1), 4-es.

Quantum Algorithm for Differential Equations

These algorithms are designed to solve high-dimensional differential equations, which describe phenomena ranging from fluid flow to heat transfer. They offer a potential exponential speedup for engineering and physics simulations that are currently limited by classical computing power.

- **Reference**: Berry, D. W., et al. (2017). Quantum algorithm for linear differential equations with exponential complexity improvement. *Communications in Mathematical Physics*, 356(3), 1057–1081.

Quantum Annealing

This method solves optimization problems by starting in a simple quantum state and slowly reducing quantum fluctuations to find the lowest-energy solution. It is often compared to "quantum tunneling," as it allows the system to pass through high-energy barriers to reach an optimal solution.

- **Reference**: Kadowaki, T., & Nishimori, H. (1998). Quantum annealing in the transverse Ising model. *Physical Review E*, 58(5), 5355.

Quantum Approximate Optimization Algorithm (QAOA)

A hybrid quantum-classical variational algorithm designed to find approximate solutions to combinatorial optimization problems like Max-Cut. It alternates between two non-commuting Hamiltonians to explore the solution space, with parameters optimized by a classical computer.

- **Reference**: Farhi, E., Goldstone, J., & Gutmann, S. (2014). A quantum approximate optimization algorithm. *arXiv preprint arXiv:1411.4028*.

Quantum Boltzmann Machine (QBM)

A quantum-enhanced neural network that learns the hidden patterns and probability structures within data by mimicking the way energy levels work in a quantum system. It is used to teach machines to recognize complex data features or to generate new data that resembles the original training set.

- **Reference**: Amin, M. H., Andriyash, E., Rolfe, J., Kulchytskyy, B., & Melko, R. (2018). Quantum Boltzmann machine. *Physical Review X*, 8(2), 021050.

Quantum Clique Finding

This algorithm searches a network to find the largest group of points in which every member is directly connected to every other member. It provides a speedup over classical brute-force searching, which is valuable for identifying clusters in social networks or biological data.

- **Reference**: Magniez, F., Santha, M., & Szegedy, M. (2007). Quantum algorithms for the triangle problem. *SIAM Journal on Computing*, 37(2), 413–424.

Quantum Counting

This algorithm estimates the total number of correct solutions in a massive search space without having to find them all. It effectively combines Grover's search with Phase Estimation to achieve a speedup for counting tasks in optimization and database management.

- **Reference**: Brassard, G., Høyer, P., & Tapp, A. (1998). Quantum counting. *Lecture Notes in Computer Science*, 1443, 820–831.

Quantum Eigenvalue Estimation

This algorithm extracts the essential numerical properties, or eigenvalues, of a matrix, which is vital for calculating energy levels in molecules. It allows researchers to solve complex physics problems that are too large for classical matrix math.

- **Reference**: Abrams, D. S., & Lloyd, S. (1999). Quantum algorithm providing exponential speedup for finding eigenvalues and eigenvectors. *Physical Review Letters*, 83(24), 5162.

Quantum Gibbs Sampling

This algorithm prepares a quantum system so that its states appear with specific probabilities according to a "temperature" setting, which is vital for simulating physics and complex statistics. It helps researchers understand how materials change state or how heat flows through a system at the atomic level.

- **Reference**: Chowdhury, A. N., & Somma, R. D. (2016). Quantum algorithms for Gibbs sampling and special properties. *Quantum Information & Computation*, 17(1–2), 41–64.

Quantum Gradient Descent

A quantum version of the popular optimization method that finds the "lowest point" or best solution of a function by evaluating gradients (slopes) in superposition. It helps accelerate the training of machine learning models and the tuning of industrial control systems.

- **Reference**: Rebentrost, P., Schuld, M., Wossnig, L., Petruccione, F., & Lloyd, S. (2019). Quantum gradient descent and Newton's method for constrained polynomial optimization. *New Journal of Physics*, 21(7), 073023.

Quantum Graph Coloring

This algorithm assigns "colors" to points on a map so that no two points connected by a line share the same color. It is often implemented as a hybrid quantum-classical task to solve complex scheduling and frequency allocation problems.

- **Reference**: Biamonte, J., et al. (2017). Quantum machine learning. *Nature*, 549(7671), 195–202.

Quantum Graph Connectivity

This algorithm quickly checks a map of nodes to determine if there is a path connecting every single point in the system. By using quantum walks, it can explore the structure of a complex graph with fewer steps than a standard computer would require.

- **Reference**: Dürr, C., Heiligman, M., Høyer, P., & Mhalla, M. (2006). Quantum query complexity of some graph problems. *SIAM Journal on Computing*, 35(6), 1310–1328.

Quantum Graph Property Testing

This algorithm checks for specific characteristics of a network shape using significantly fewer queries than a classical computer. It is essential for analyzing the structure of massive graphs, such as global power grids or biological neural networks.

- **Reference**: Ambainis, A., & Childs, A. M. (2005). Quantum algorithms for fixed-point search and graph problems. *Proceedings of the 22nd Annual IEEE Conference on Computational Complexity*, 248–259.

Quantum Hamiltonian Path

This algorithm determines if there is a single path that visits every node in a network exactly once. It uses quantum interference to rule out incorrect paths much faster than classical trial-and-error methods.

- **Reference**: Nielsen, M. A., & Chuang, I. L. (2010). *Quantum Computation and Quantum Information*. Cambridge University Press.

Quantum Independent Set

This algorithm identifies the largest possible collection of points in a network such that no two points in the set are directly connected. It is typically solved using variational quantum circuits that explore many possible combinations simultaneously to find the best arrangement.

- **Reference**: Farhi, E., Goldstone, J., & Gutmann, S. (2014). A quantum approximate optimization algorithm. *arXiv preprint arXiv:1411.4028.*

Quantum Interior Point Method

This algorithm solves complicated optimization problems with specific constraints by using quantum linear solvers to navigate the interior of an "allowed" solution space. It is particularly useful for financial portfolio balancing and large-scale logistics where many rules must be followed.

- **Reference**: Kerenidis, I., & Prakash, A. (2020). A quantum interior point method for LPs and SDPs. *ACM Transactions on Quantum Computing*, 1(1), 1–32.

Quantum Knapsack Problem

This algorithm selects the most valuable combination of items to fit into a container without exceeding its weight limit. It utilizes quantum-enhanced optimization to solve this common resource-allocation problem more effectively than classical heuristics.

- **Reference**: Akhalwaya, I. Y., et al. (2022). A quantum-inspired method for the knapsack problem. *Quantum Information Processing*, 21(1), 1–25.

Quantum Least Squares

A quantum method for finding the "best fit" line or curve through a set of data points by solving the underlying matrix equations exponentially faster than classical computers. This is a core tool for data scientists performing regression analysis on massive datasets.

- **Reference**: Wiebe, N., Kapoor, A., & Svore, K. M. (2012). Quantum algorithms for nearest-neighbor methods for supervised and unsupervised learning. *Quantum Information & Computation*, 15(3–4), 316–350.

Quantum Linear Differential Equations

This approach simulates the behavior of systems governed by linear dynamics more efficiently by mapping the equations onto a quantum state and evolving it. It offers a significant speedup for engineers and physicists studying wave propagation or heat transfer in large-scale materials.

- **Reference**: Childs, A. M., & Liu, J. P. (2020). High-precision quantum algorithms for partial differential equations. *Communications in Mathematical Physics*, 375(2), 1427–1467.

Quantum Linear Systems Algorithm (aka HHL)

HHL solves large systems of linear equations ($\boldsymbol{Ax} = \boldsymbol{b}$) using quantum logic to perform the computation in a way that can be exponentially faster than classical solvers. It is a foundational tool for future applications in fluid dynamics and weather modeling.

- **Reference**: Harrow, A. W., Hassidim, A., & Lloyd, S. (2009). Quantum algorithm for linear systems of equations. *Physical Review Letters*, 103(15), 150502.

Quantum Matching Problems

This algorithm efficiently pairs elements from two different groups (like jobs to workers or buyers to sellers) to maximize total benefit. It uses quantum superposition to evaluate many possible pairing combinations simultaneously, significantly reducing the computational time for market matching.

- **Reference**: Childs, A. M., & Kothari, R. (2012). Quantum query complexity of minor-closed graph properties. *SIAM Journal on Computing*, 41(5), 1316–1342.

Quantum Matrix Multiplication

A fundamental procedure that allows a quantum computer to multiply two massive grids of numbers at once by encoding them into quantum states and performing rotations. This is the engine behind many other quantum advantages, including faster machine learning and more detailed physics simulations.

- **Reference**: Childs, A. M., Kothari, R., & Somma, R. D. (2017). Quantum algorithm for systems of linear equations with exponentially improved dependence on precision. *SIAM Journal on Computing*, 46(6), 1920–1950.

Quantum Maximum Finding

A variation of the search process that efficiently identifies the largest value in a dataset with significantly fewer evaluations than traditional linear scans. It utilizes probability amplitude amplification to make the maximum value the most likely outcome of a measurement.

- **Reference**: Ahuja, A., & Kapoor, S. (1999). A quantum algorithm for finding the maximum. *arXiv preprint quant-ph/9911082*.

Quantum Maximum Flow

This algorithm identifies the greatest amount of "traffic" or data that can move from a starting point to an ending point through a network with limited capacities. It leverages quantum search techniques to find paths more efficiently than classical methods.

- **Reference**: Ambainis, A. (2007). Quantum walk algorithm for element distinctness. *SIAM Journal on Computing*, 37(1), 210–239.

Quantum Median Finding

This method determines the middle value of a dataset by leveraging quantum counting and search techniques to avoid the high cost of fully sorting the data. It achieves faster results by estimating the ranks of elements using quantum superposition.

- **Reference**: Nayak, A., & Wu, F. (1999). The quantum complexity of approximating the median. *Proceedings of the 31st Annual ACM Symposium on Theory of Computing*, 384–393.

Quantum Metropolis Sampling

Inspired by a classical method used in physics, this algorithm prepares and samples from the "equilibrium" or most stable states of a physical system at a specific temperature. It is essential for researchers trying to understand how materials behave under various thermal conditions.

- **Reference**: Temme, K., et al. (2011). Quantum Metropolis sampling. *Nature*, 471(7336), 87–90.

Quantum Minimum Finding

This algorithm finds the smallest element in an unsorted list by building Achlioptas's search to provide a quadratic speedup over classical brute-force search. It works by repeatedly using a quantum threshold to narrow down the smallest value through interference.

- **Reference**: Dürr, C., & Hoyer, P. (1996). A quantum algorithm for finding the minimum. *arXiv preprint quant-ph/9607014.*

Quantum Monte Carlo Speedup

This technique uses a method called "Amplitude Estimation" to provide a faster way to calculate average outcomes in random scenarios, such as predicting financial market risks or weather patterns. It offers a quadratic speedup over classical sampling methods.

- **Reference**: Montanaro, A. (2015). Quantum speedup of Monte Carlo methods. *Proceedings of the Royal Society A: Mathematical, Physical and Engineering Sciences*, 471(2181), 20150301.

Quantum Network Flows

This optimization algorithm determines the most efficient way to move "traffic" or resources through a network without exceeding the capacity of any single path. It is used to optimize the flow of oil through pipelines or data through telecommunications infrastructure.

- **Reference**: Ambainis, A. (2007). Quantum walk algorithm for element distinctness. *SIAM Journal on Computing*, 37(1), 210–239.

Quantum Order Finding

This algorithm identifies the smallest positive integer ***r*** such that a number raised to the ***r***-th power is 1 in modular arithmetic. It is the critical "engine" inside Shor's algorithm that enables factoring large prime numbers.

- **Reference**: Shor, P. W. (1994). Algorithms for quantum computation: discrete logarithms and factoring. *Proceedings of the 35th Annual Symposium on Foundations of Computer Science*, 124–134.

Quantum PageRank

Based on the Google PageRank concept, this algorithm uses quantum walks to identify the most important or "influential" nodes in a massive network. It provides a more nuanced ranking of web pages or social media nodes by exploiting quantum interference.

- **Reference**: Paparo, G. D., & Martin-Delgado, M. A. (2012). Google in a quantum network. *Scientific Reports*, 2(1), 444.

Quantum Phase Estimation (QPE)

QPE estimates the phase (or eigenvalue) associated with a specific operation, acting as a core subroutine for nearly all advanced quantum algorithms. It translates internal quantum timing information into readable digital values.

- **Reference**: Kitaev, A. Y. (1995). Quantum measurements and the Abelian Stabilizer Problem. *arXiv preprint quant-ph/9511026.*

Quantum Principal Component Analysis (QPCA)

QPCA identifies the most significant patterns and structures within massive, high-dimensional datasets. By representing data as quantum states, it can reveal correlations that would take classical computers an impractical amount of time to find.

- **Reference**: Lloyd, S., Mohseni, M., & Rebentrost, P. (2014). Quantum principal component analysis. *Nature Physics*, 10(9), 631–633.

Quantum Recommendation Systems

This algorithm analyzes massive datasets to predict a user's preferences, such as which movie they might want to watch next, by treating the data as a large quantum matrix. It provides an exponential speedup in processing the underlying patterns compared to classical systems.

- **Reference**: Kerenidis, I., & Prakash, A. (2016). Quantum recommendation systems. *arXiv preprint arXiv:1603.08675.*

Quantum Rejection Sampling

This technique improves upon classical "hit-or-miss" sampling by using quantum superposition to accept or reject proposed data points more efficiently. It provides a faster way to obtain samples from a desired target distribution.

- **Reference**: Ozols, M., Roetteler, M., & Roland, J. (2013). Quantum rejection sampling. *ACM Transactions on Computation Theory*, 5(3), 1–33.

Quantum Sampling

This broad category of algorithms allows a quantum computer to generate data points from incredibly complex probability distributions that are too dense for classical computers to handle efficiently. It serves as a fundamental tool for quantum machine learning.

- **Reference**: Montanaro, A. (2015). Quantum speedup of Monte Carlo methods. *Proceedings of the Royal Society A*, 471(2181), 20150301.

Quantum SAT (Satisfiability)

This algorithm determines if there is a way to assign "true" or "false" values to a set of logical statements so that the entire formula remains true. The quantum version uses amplitude amplification to find these solutions faster.

- **Reference**: Ambainis, A. (2004). Quantum search algorithms. *SIGACT News*, 35(2), 22–35.

Quantum Semidefinite Programming (SDP)

A powerful optimization framework that solves problems involving many interacting constraints by representing them as matrices and finding the best way to satisfy all of them simultaneously.

- **Reference**: Brandão, F. G., & Svore, K. M. (2017). Quantum speed-ups for semidefinite programming. *Proceedings of the 58th Annual IEEE Symposium on Foundations of Computer Science*, 303–314.

Quantum Shortest Paths

Using quantum search and walk techniques, this algorithm finds the quickest route between two points in a massive, complex map. It provides a quadratic speedup over classical navigation algorithms.

- **Reference**: Dürr, C., Heiligman, M., Høyer, P., & Mhalla, M. (2006). Quantum query complexity of some graph problems. *SIAM Journal on Computing*, 35(6), 1310–1328.

Quantum Simulation of Chemistry

These algorithms model the complex interactions of electrons and nuclei in molecules to predict chemical reactions and material properties. This is a primary driver for using quantum computers to accelerate drug and material discovery.

- **Reference**: Kassal, I., et al. (2011). Simulating chemistry on computers. *Annual Review of Physical Chemistry*, 62, 185–207.

Quantum Simulation of Lattice Models

This approach uses qubits to simulate particles arranged on a grid, helping physicists study how magnetism, electricity, and other properties emerge in solid materials.

- **Reference**: Georgescu, I. M., Ashhab, S., & Nori, F. (2014). Quantum simulation. *Reviews of Modern Physics*, 86(1), 153.

Quantum Support Vector Machine (QSVM)

QSVM uses quantum circuits to perform high-speed classification, mapping data into a complex "quantum feature space" to find boundaries between groups that are invisible to classical machines.

- **Reference**: Rebentrost, P., Mohseni, M., & Lloyd, S. (2014). Quantum support vector machine for big data classification. *Physical Review Letters*, 113(13), 130503.

Quantum Systems of Differential Equations

This algorithm provides a way to find the state of a complex system over time by solving multiple linked differential equations simultaneously using quantum linear algebra.

- **Reference**: Berry, D. W. (2014). High-order quantum algorithm for solving linear differential equations. *Journal of Physics A: Mathematical and Theoretical*, 47(10), 105301.

Quantum Traveling Salesman Problem (Q-TSP)

This algorithm searches for the shortest possible route that visits a list of locations exactly once and returns to the start. It uses quantum optimization to navigate complex route landscapes more efficiently.

- **Reference**: Srinivasan, K., et al. (2018). Efficient combinatorial optimization using quantum computing. *Scientific Reports*, 8(1), 1–13.

Quantum Walk (Continuous-Time)

This algorithm allows a quantum state to evolve smoothly and continuously over time across a graph according to the Schrödinger equation. It is used to design efficient search algorithms and simulate constantly changing physical systems.

- **Reference**: Farhi, E., & Gutmann, S. (1998). Quantum computation and decision trees. *Physical Review A*, 58(2), 915.

Quantum Walk (Discrete-Time)

The discrete-time quantum walk uses a "coin" qubit to determine movement directions at each step, exploring multiple paths on a graph simultaneously via superposition, spreading faster than a classical random walk.

- **Reference**: Aharonov, Y., Davidovich, L., & Zagury, N. (1993). Quantum random walks. *Physical Review A*, 48(2), 1687.

Shor's Algorithm

A landmark quantum algorithm that factors large integers and solves discrete logarithms in polynomial time. Its ability to solve these problems efficiently poses a direct threat to modern public-key cryptography, such as RSA.

- **Reference**: Shor, P. W. (1994). Algorithms for quantum computation: Discrete logarithms and factoring. *Proceedings of the 35th Annual Symposium on Foundations of Computer Science*, 124–134.

Simon's Algorithm

An algorithm that finds a hidden period in a black-box function, demonstrating an exponential speedup over any classical probabilistic method. It directly inspired the development of Shor's factoring algorithm.

- **Reference**: Simon, D. R. (1997). On the power of quantum computation. *SIAM Journal on Computing*, 26(5), 1474–1483.

Solving Exponential Congruences

This quantum algorithm solves equations in which variables appear in exponents and must satisfy a modular relation. It utilizes quantum parallelism to find solutions significantly faster than classical index-calculus methods.

- **Reference**: Shor, P. W. (1997). Polynomial-time algorithms for prime factorization and discrete logarithms on a quantum computer. *SIAM Journal on Computing*, 26(5), 1484–1509.

Solovay-Kitaev Algorithm

A constructive algorithm used to approximate any arbitrary single-qubit unitary gate using a finite set of universal gates. It is crucial for ensuring logic gates can be compiled into hardware-specific sets with high precision.

- **Reference**: Dawson, C. M., & Nielsen, M. A. (2005). The Solovay-Kitaev algorithm. *Quantum Information & Computation*, 6(1), 81–95.

Spatial Search

Spatial search is used to find a specific target item hidden within a physical grid or multi-dimensional arrangement of data. It relies on a quantum walk that spreads across the grid to locate the target faster than classical search.

- **Reference**: Childs, A. M., & Goldstone, J. (2004). Spatial search by quantum walk. *Physical Review A*, 70(2), 022314.

Superdense Coding Algorithm

A quantum communication protocol that allows a sender to transmit two classical bits of information by sending only one qubit, provided an entangled pair is pre-shared. It demonstrates the utility of entanglement for increasing communication capacity.

- **Reference**: Bennett, C. H., & Wiesner, S. J. (1992). Communication via one- and two-particle operators on Einstein-Podolsky-Rosen states. *Physical Review Letters*, 69(20), 2881.

Triangle Finding

This graph-theoretic algorithm searches for three pairwise-connected nodes. It utilizes quantum walk techniques to find these structures more efficiently than traditional search methods.

- **Reference**: Magniez, F., Santha, M., & Szegedy, M. (2007). Quantum algorithms for the triangle problem. *SIAM Journal on Computing*, 37(2), 413–424.

Unit Group

This algorithm computes the structure of invertible elements (units) within a given number system. It uses quantum techniques to efficiently find these building blocks, solving a fundamental problem in algebraic number theory.

- **Reference**: van Dam, W., & Hallgren, S. (2000). Efficient quantum algorithms for shift-invariant problems. *Proceedings of the 41st Annual Symposium on Foundations of Computer Science*, 176–185.

Variational Quantum Eigensolver (VQE)

A hybrid algorithm used primarily in chemistry that adjusts a quantum circuit like a set of dials until the system reaches its lowest energy configuration. This allows for molecular simulation without requiring fully error-corrected hardware.

- **Reference**: Peruzzo, A., et al. (2014). A variational eigenvalue solver on a photonic quantum processor. *Nature Communications*, 5(1), 4213.

Table 1: A category-wise illustration of algorithms and their strategic applications

Category	Algorithm Name	Strategic Application
Algebraic & Number Theory	Shor's Algorithm	Factoring large integers; threat to RSA encryption.
	Discrete Logarithm	Solving exponentiation problems; threat to ECC security.
	Abelian Hidden Subgroup Problem	Unified framework for finding patterns in commutative symmetries.
	Pell's Equation	Solving quadratic Diophantine equations.
	Unit Group/Class Group	Structural analysis of algebraic number systems.
	Primality Proving	Efficiently certifying large prime numbers.
	Gauss Sum Estimation	Approximation for number theory and physics.
	Solving Exponential Congruences	Solving modular equations with variable exponents.
Search & Database	Grover's Algorithm	Quadratic speedup for unstructured database searching.
	Quantum Minimum/ Maximum Finding	Locating extreme values in unsorted lists.
	Quantum Median Finding	Efficiently finding middle values in a dataset.

Category	Algorithm Name	Strategic Application
	Amplitude Amplification	Generalizing Grover's mechanism to improve probability.
	Collision Finding	Finding identical outputs for different inputs in security.
	Element Distinctness	Identifying duplicate items in large datasets.
	Spatial Search	Searching grids or multi-dimensional data arrangements.
Optimization	Adiabatic Quantum Optimization (AQO)	Slow evolution to find global minimum (rest state).
	Quantum Annealing	Tunneling through energy barriers to find optimal solutions.
	QAOA (Quantum Approximate Optimization)	Hybrid near-term solutions for combinatorial problems (e.g., Max-Cut).
	Quantum Traveling Salesman Problem	Shortest route optimization for logistics.
	Quantum Knapsack Problem	Resource allocation under weight/capacity constraints.
	Quantum SAT (Satisfiability)	Assigning logic values to satisfy complex formulas.

Category	Algorithm Name	Strategic Application
	Quantum Interior Point Method	Constrained optimization for finance and logistics.
	Quantum Semidefinite Programming (SDP)	Solving optimization with multiple interacting constraints.
Linear Algebra & Big Data	HHL Algorithm	Solving massive systems of linear equations (Ax=b).
	Quantum Matrix Multiplication	Engine for accelerating high-dimensional math.
	Quantum Principal Component Analysis (QPCA)	Finding significant patterns in high-dimensional data.
	Quantum Support Vector Machine (QSVM)	High-speed classification in quantum feature space.
	Quantum Least Squares	Best-fit analysis for regression and data science.
	Quantum PageRank	Ranking influence in networks using interference.
	Quantum Recommendation Systems	Predicting user preferences via matrix processing.
Simulation & Physics	Hamiltonian Simulation	Modeling how molecules and materials change over time.
	Variational Quantum Eigensolver (VQE)	Hybrid ground-state energy calculation for chemistry.

Category	Algorithm Name	Strategic Application
	Quantum Simulation (Chemistry/ Lattice)	Modeling atomic interactions and solid-state materials.
	Quantum Eigenvalue Estimation	Extracting numerical properties for molecular energy levels.
	Boson/Gaussian Boson Sampling	Specialized tasks demonstrating "quantum supremacy."
	Differential Equations (Linear/ Systems)	Modeling fluid flow, heat transfer, and wave propagation.
Graph & Logic	Quantum Walk (Discrete/ Continuous)	Fast traversal of complex graphs and decision trees.
	Graph Isomorphism	Determining if two complex networks share the same structure.
	Triangle Finding/ Clique Finding	Identifying structural clusters and cliques in networks.
	NAND Tree/ Formula Evaluation	Fast evaluation of complex logical decision trees.
	Quantum Network Flows/Shortest Paths	Optimizing resource movement through infrastructure.

Category	Algorithm Name	Strategic Application
	Quantum Graph Connectivity	Checking if paths connect all points in a system.
Communication & Sampling	BB84 Protocol	Physics-based secure Quantum Key Distribution (QKD).
	Superdense Coding Algorithm	Doubling communication capacity using entanglement.
	Amplitude Estimation/Monte Carlo	Accelerated risk analysis and average outcome calculation.
	Quantum Gibbs/ Metropolis Sampling	Simulating stable physical states at specific temperatures.
	Quantum Rejection Sampling	Efficient data sampling from complex distributions.
	Quantum Counting	Estimating number of solutions in massive search spaces.
Hardware & Control	Solovay-Kitaev Algorithm	Compiling logical gates into hardware-specific sets.
	GRAPE Algorithm	Iterative optimization of high-fidelity control pulses.
	CRAB Algorithm	Randomized basis optimization for experimental control.

About the Authors

Sanjana Rajeshkumar Gupta is an AI Scientist at the Center of Excellence – Oil, Gas, and Energy (CoE-OGE) at IIT Bombay, where she focuses on deploying advanced AI frameworks in high-stakes industrial environments. Specialized in the intersection of data science and complex energy systems, her work is central to modernizing legacy industrial processes through intelligent automation. She holds a Master's in Data Science from The Institute of Science, Dr. Homi Bhabha State University, Mumbai. With a deep technical background and a focus on the practical application of emerging technologies, she contributes a vital research perspective to the development of quantum-ready strategies for the next generation of energy security and industrial efficiency.

Dr. Satyam Priyadarshy is the Visionary CEO of Reignite Future and a pioneer in the strategic application of exponential technologies. A globally recognized transformational leader, he holds the distinction of being the first Chief Data Scientist in the Oil and Gas industry. With a career spanning leadership roles at Halliburton, AOL, and Acxiom, Dr. Priyadarshy bridges the gap between complex science and industrial reality. As a Visiting Chair Professor at IIT Bombay and a prolific innovator with multiple patents, he has delivered over 150 global keynotes on the future of Quantum Mechanics, AI, and Digital Disruption. Recognized by Forbes India and the AI 100 as a top influencer in digital innovation, he serves as a strategic advisor to emerging technology firms worldwide, helping leaders navigate the transition to the intelligent machine age.

Global Quantum Intelligence (GQI) is the premier strategic advisory firm driving transformation within the quantum economy. Through a focus on growth strategy, leadership evolution, and market expansion, GQI empowers organizations to move from quantum awareness to quantum readiness. The GQI Platform serves as the definitive command center for the quantum transition. Engineered specifically for decision-makers, it integrates curated global data, dynamic analytics, and expert insights into a single, unified interface. It is the intelligence layer required to navigate the complexities of the quantum landscape with precision and foresight.